THE PIANO SOLOS OF
RICHARD CLAYDERMAN
Music of Love

T0045575

7777 W. BLUEMOUND RD. P.O. BOX 13819 MILWAUKEE, WI 53213

Visit Hal Leonard Online at
www.halleonard.com

BALLADE POUR ADELINE

Music by PAUL DE SENNEVILLE

Slowly

3

BARCAROLLE

Music by J. OFFENBACH
Arranged by O. TOUSSAINT/G. SALESSES

Moderately

7

DON'T CRY FOR ME ARGENTINA

(From the opera "EVITA")

Lyric by TIM RICE
Music by ANDREW LLOYD WEBBER

FEELINGS
(¿DIME?)

English words and music by MORRIS ALBERT
Spanish lyric by THOMAS FUNDORA

Slowly

13

LA VIE EN ROSE

French Words by EDITH PIAF
English Words by MACK DAVID
Music by LOUIGY

GUANTANAMERA

Original lyrics and music
by JOSE FERNANDEZ DIAZ (JOSEITO FERNANDEZ)
Music adaptation by PETE SEEGER
Lyric adaptation by HECTOR ANGULO,
based on a poem by JOSE MARTI

LIEBESTRAUM

Music by FRANZ LISZT
Arranged by O. TOUSSAINT/G. SALESSES

Moderato

LARA'S THEME

By MAURICE JARRE

Andante

LOVE IS A MANY-SPLENDORED THING

Words by PAUL FRANCIS WEBSTER
Music by SAMMY FAIN

Slowly, ad lib.

Rhythmically

LOVE IS BLUE
(L'AMOUR EST BLEU)

English Lyric by BRIAN BLACKBURN
Original French Lyric by PIERRE COUR
Music by ANDRE POPP

Andante

LOVE STORY

Lyric by CARL SIGMAN
Music by FRANCIS LAI

Cantabile

MEDLEY
La Mer (Beyond the Sea) - Yesterday - Till

"LA MER"
Moderately fast

LA MER
By CHARLES TRENET & ALBERT LASRY

"YESTERDAY"
Quietly

YESTERDAY

Words and Music by JOHN LENNON and PAUL McCARTNEY

"TILL"
Moderately

TILL
Words by CARL SIGMAN
Music by CHARLES DANVERS

Copyright © 1956 & 1957 by Chappell & Co., Inc.

MOON RIVER

Words by JOHNNY MERCER
Music by HENRY MANCINI

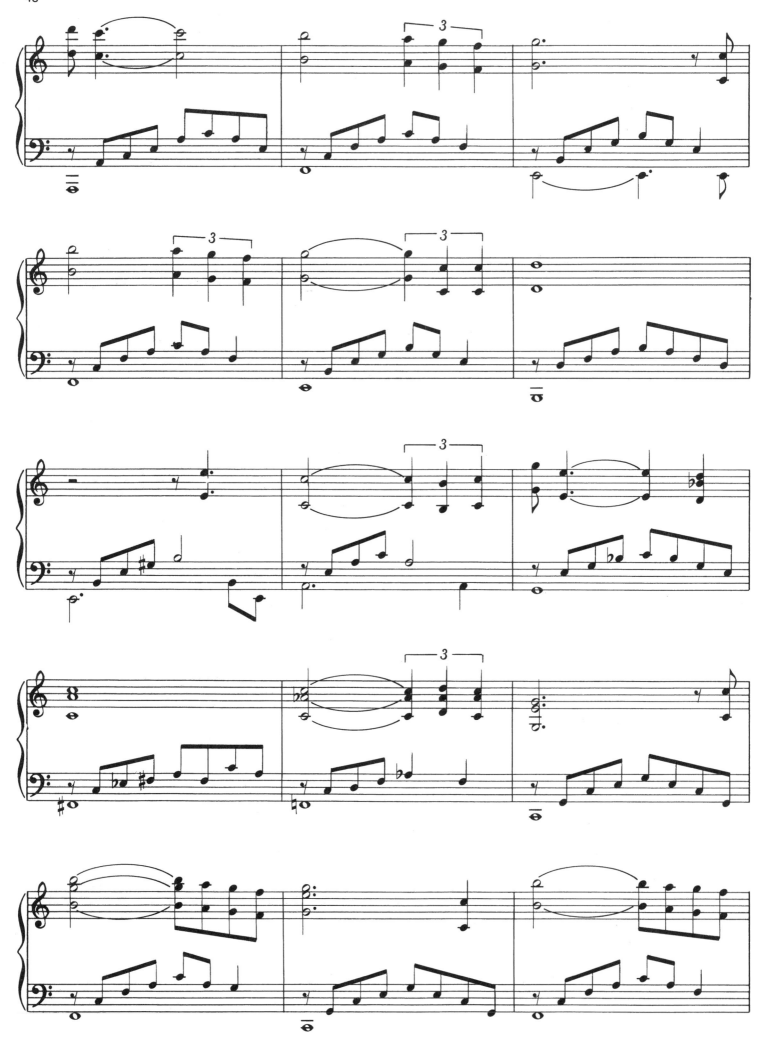

SONATE AU CLAIR DE LUNE
(MOONLIGHT SONATA)

Music by LUDWIG VAN BEETHOVEN
Arranged by O. TOUSSAINT/G. SALESSES

Adagio sostenuto

TRÄUMEREI

Music by ROBERT SCHUMANN
Arranged by O. TOUSSAINT/G. SALESSES

Slowly, with expression

ROMEO AND JULIET

Words by LARRY KUSIK
and EDDIE SNYDER
Music by NINO ROTA

STRANGERS IN THE NIGHT

Words by CHARLES SINGLETON
and EDDIE SNYDER
Music by BERT KAEMPFERT

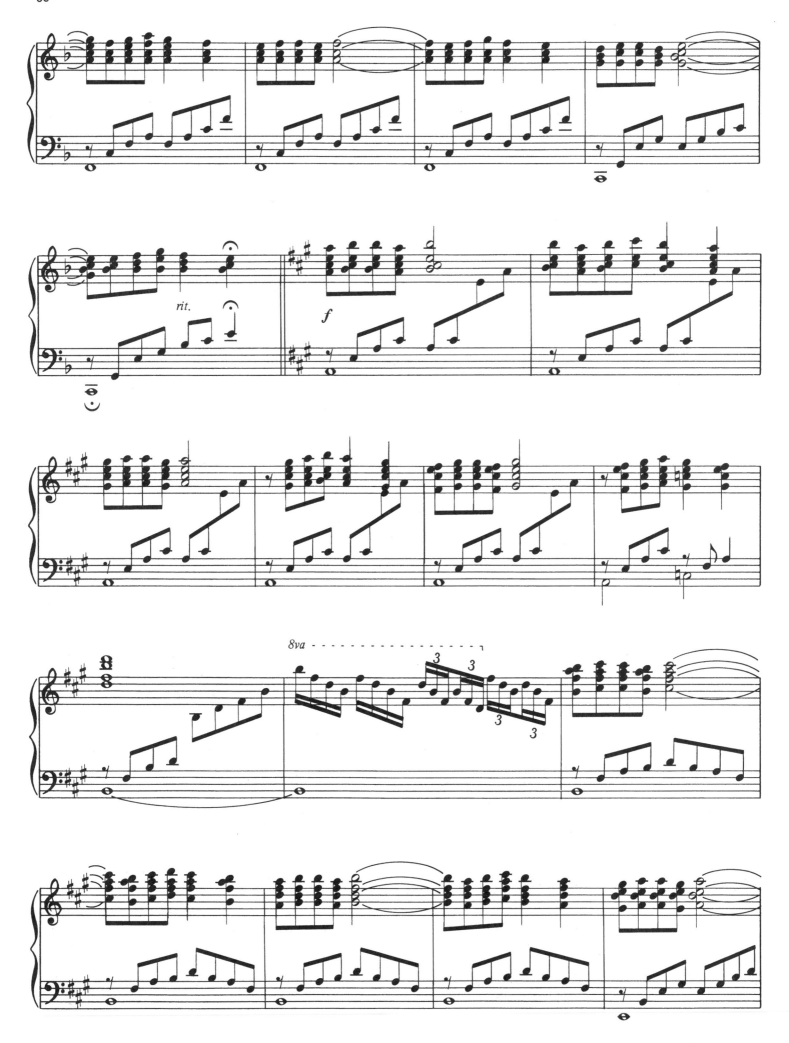

SERENADE

Music by FRANZ SCHUBERT
Arranged by O. TOUSSAINT/G. SALESSES